LEVEL
1

Meerkats

Laura Marsh

NATIONAL
GEOGRAPHIC

Washington, D.C.

For Matthew and Eliza—L. F. M.

The publisher and author gratefully acknowledge the expert review of this book by Peter Santema of the University of Cambridge and the Kalahari Meerkat Project.

Paperback ISBN: 978-1-4263-1342-4
Library ISBN: 978-1-4263-1343-1

Book design by YAY! Design

Photo credits

Cover, Beverly Joubert/National Geographic Stock; 1, Evan Chu/National Geographic My Shot; 2, Graham Smith/National Geographic Your Shot; 4–5, Flickr RF/Getty Images; 6, Renato Pejkovic/Shutterstock; 7, Jason Finlay/National Geographic My Shot; 8, Mattias Klum/National Geographic/Getty Images; 10, Mattias Klum/National Geographic Stock; 11 (UP), Anthony West/National Geographic My Shot; 11 (UPCTR), vblinov/Shutterstock; 11 (LOCTR), Jared Offutt/National Geographic My Shot; 11 (LO), formiktopus/Shutterstock; 12, Simon King/naturepl.com; 13, Martin Harvey/Getty Images; 14, Martin Harvey/Kimball Stock; 15, Susan McConnell/National Geographic My Shot; 16, Tim Jackson/Getty Images; 17, Mattias Klum/National Geographic Stock; 18–19, Marguerite Smits Van Oyen/naturepl.com; 20, Solvin Zankl/naturepl.com; 21, Simon King/naturepl.com; 22, Chaikovskiy Igor/Shutterstock; 22 (UPLE), Renato Pejkovic/Shutterstock; 22 (UPRT), Colette3/Shutterstock; 22 (LO), John Antoniadis/National Geographic Your Shot; 23 (UP), Andalucia Plus Image bank/Alamy; 23 (LOLE), Heinrich van den Berg/Getty Images; 23 (LORT), Vincent Grafhorst/Foto Natura/Minden Pictures; 23 (LOCTR), Maslov Dmitry/Shutterstock; 24, Jack Bishop/Alamy; 25, Mattias Klum/National Geographic Stock; 26–27, Martin Harvey/Gallo Images/Getty Images; 28–29, AnetaPics/Shutterstock; 30 (LE), Martin Hughes/National Geographic My Shot; 30 (RT), Jared Offutt/National Geographic My Shot; 31 (UPLE), Martin Harvey/Getty Images; 31 (UPRT), Sharon Carone/National Geographic My Shot; 31 (LOLE), vblinov/Shutterstock; 31 (LORT), Tony Britton/National Geographic My Shot; 32 (UPLE), Donald Healy/National Geographic My Shot; 32 (UPRT), Vincent Grafhorst/Foto Natura/Minden Pictures; 32 (LOLE), Renato Pejkovic/Shutterstock; 32 (LORT), Daryl Balfour/Gallo Images/Getty Images; top borders and Wild Word boxes, Shutterstock

Table of Contents

What Are They?

They have fun, just like you.
They work, play, and rest, too.

They dig in the sand
and lie in the sun.
Most often you'll find
more than one!

What are they? Meerkats!

All About Meerkats

Meerkats are funny to look at.
Sometimes they stand on their back
legs. Their paws hang down in front.

Meerkats belong to the mongoose
family. They live in the desert.
It is hot and dry there.

yellow mongoose

Wild Word

MONGOOSE: A furry
animal with a long
body and tail. It lives
in Africa and Asia.

Terrific Tunnels

A meerkat's home is under the ground. It is called a burrow.

Long tunnels lead to rooms. Meerkats sleep in the burrow at night.

Wild Word

BURROW: A hole or tunnel that an animal digs to use as a home

On the Menu

Meerkats eat many things. Their favorite foods are beetles and scorpions (SKOR-pee-uns). They like lizards and grubs, too.

scorpion

beetle

lizard

grubs

How do meerkats find most of their food? They dig for it!

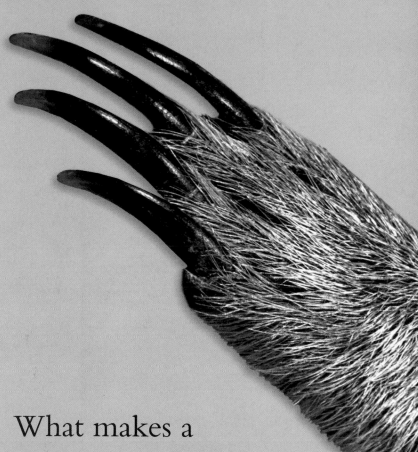

What makes a
super-fast digger?
Long, curvy
claws and four
digging paws.

Big Family

Meerkats live in a big group.
A few families live all together.
The group is called a mob.

Meerkats work and rest together.
They also play and sleep together.

A Job to Do

Every meerkat has
a job. Each job helps
the group.

babysitter

Babysitters

Most of the adults are out hunting. Young meerkats need care. So babysitters watch over them.

Babysitters comfort little ones.

Guards

Guards watch for predators
(PRED-uh-turs). They stand on
a hill, rock, or tree.

Wild Word

PREDATOR: An
animal that hunts and
eats other animals

The guards make a loud peeping
sound. This warns the others.
Look out!

Teachers

Teachers show young meerkats how to find a meal. They show them how to eat it, too.

Feeders

Babies need milk. Mothers and other females in the mob feed the babies. The feeders take turns.

A female feeds young meerkats.

7 Cool Facts About Meerkats

1

Meerkats sometimes share their homes with yellow mongooses (above).

2

Meerkats have great noses! They can smell food that's under the sand.

3

Meerkats like to snuggle. It keeps them warm. And they like to stick together.

4

Meerkats lie in the sun
to warm up.

5

A meerkat can dig
hundreds of holes in
one morning!

6

A meerkat burrow usually
has about 15
rooms.

7

A meerkat is about the
size of a squirrel.

Pups

Meerkat babies are called pups.
They are born with their
eyes closed.

The pups grow fast! They run
and dig. Soon the pups will be
all grown up.

Staying Safe

Meerkats know what to do when a predator arrives. Sometimes, they stand together. They show their teeth and hiss. This might scare off the predator.

Other times, meerkats just run. They hide in a bolt hole.

Wild Word

BOLT HOLE: A hole in the ground where meerkats run to hide from danger. It's wide enough to fit many meerkats at once.

Meerkats are fun to watch.
But what's extra special
about them?

Meerkats help each other!
Sticking together keeps them safe.

What in the World?

These pictures are up-close views of things in a meerkat's world. Use the hints to figure out what's in the pictures. Answers are on page 31.

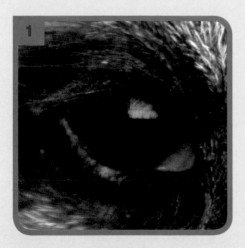

HINT: Meerkats have black circles around these.

HINT: An animal with bumpy skin that meerkats like to eat

WORD BANK

claws	eyes	beetle	fur	lizard	nose

HINT: These help meerkats make holes.

HINT: Hair that covers an animal

HINT: A favorite snack for meerkats

HINT: Meerkats have one. So do you.

Answers: 1. eyes, 2. lizard, 3. claws, 4. fur, 5. beetle, 6. nose

BOLT HOLE: A hole in the ground where meerkats run to hide from danger. It's wide enough to fit many meerkats at once.

BURROW: A hole or tunnel that an animal digs to use as a home

MONGOOSE: A furry animal with a long body and tail. It lives in Africa and Asia.

PREDATOR: An animal that hunts and eats other animals